Ça Existe!

Lauri Robertson

SPUYTEN DUYVIL
NEW YORK CITY

Cover photographs by the author:
Front— Flower Fossil, *Galerie de Paléontologie et d'Anatomie comparée,* Paris, 2018
Back—Leaf Imprints, Boston, 2019

The lucid, tender poems in *Ça Existe*, Lauri Robertson's fifth collection from Spuyten Duyvil, continue to unfold as a series of musings that proceed, literally, from a tower in the Loire valley, the "Garden of France." From her new home, the poet as expatriate psychotherapist-in-retirement addresses the predicament of aging "Boomers" bearing witness to a brutally humanized but undying planet. In the words of the poet: "The funeral parlor next to the bar / is for sale. Actually, the bar is too." We take it from there, and move onward.

André Spears, author of *From the Lost Land, I-XIII*

Lauri Robertson writes crisp verse, but as in wine descriptions, such terms are "really just moods." Here are more moods: a bright room with huge windows that wash all the shadows away ("Is an empty room a preview / or from where we came?"). Not that Robertson's lines are without darkness. But they find a home in figures of thought or in sparks of keen wit rather than self-indulgent posturing. This is a salutary restraint: "I want to live poor. Not poor poor / but rich with modesty" (there's a hint of irony: no one wants to live poor poor, just as the poet's economy of means disguises a wealth of them at her disposal). "I hate metaphor. I want only the actual / unembellished," she writes; "Speak clearly," and she seems to. But this is deceptive work: after all, "Whose language might be understood?" It's all in the details...

Alexander Dickow, author of *Appetites and Caramboles*

In Lauri Robertson's vital 5th volume, her voice is both softer and more penetrating. Bemused, confident and philosophical, she subtly integrates questions of the ages and painful themes of our time. With characteristic wit, gravity can be light and frivolity heavy, but always intimate and keenly observed. These are clear-eyed poems even for people who don't like poetry. Memory, time passing, mortality, external and internal landscapes, animals and euphony Existe!

Peggy Tramposch

ALSO BY LAURI ROBERTSON

An Æsthetic of Stone
In Concert
Where Do the Memories Go?
Après

for Barbara DiMauro

CONTENTS

III SECOND BLOOM

I

ATTENTIONS

APPLE TREE

Can you get truth
from an apple tree?
No, you can get apples.

They hang, they fall
all colors and colors between.
Their weight carries no gravity
their cider neither rot nor core.

Do you look to the sky
or ground to find them
in abundance?

ATMOSPHERE

There's need for atmosphere, something
to breathe, evoke and spirit, to create
what there's no mind for, exude.
Skies, storms, antiquity. Landscape.

The fields are fallow again
small green shoots a bedding crop
to veil the groomed earth.
The sun inescapable over the plateau
immeasurably above the river valleys.

Sacred nothing. Just peaceful nothing.
Not even memory of what was sown
sprouted, admired, scythed.

A farmer must.
A farmer must love dust.

The clouds are high.
They bloom without metaphor.
They are the metaphor
and darkness invades them.

A beautiful pheasant hops from a trench
escapes us, thankfully. Then two.
How rarely we see them now—
red face and white ring, bobbing tail.

Miraculous boredom of endless fields
an attachment to land
so profound it becomes fantasy
as it's always been.

Darkening clouds and rain
thankfully, at last. Night, inevitable
but to be undone. Your preference
for light inescapable.

Romanticize. Lyricize.
But these are eternal.
Seek them, wed them.
Let them forgive us.

BETWEEN

First you discover the Atlantic Ocean
then the Pacific. They're similar
but not the same.

There are mountains, then valleys
attached, but different, very different
but attached. Always driven to discover—

Why? Why not work or rest
in peace? With small bounty, love.
Why search when there's nothing to find?

           *

Always wanting a perch from afar
to see minutiae magnified
the world to tell its rare stillness
the slender silver lamp, the chair
lyrical ceiling rosette. They mean
something, to whom?

His mother's silver in the drawer
opulent, stuffed, ridiculous
a banquet, a buried fantasy
meaning something beyond.

*

Here is the plateau between rivers
each valley steep. I like the smaller one
better, modest water, compact shores
and closer to our village.

You have to go down a long way
almost from the clouds
from this flat place
we emerge to on return.

So far above the highest flow.
Down, down. *Go Down Moses.*
Or we'll stay up, cheerful
with the grapes and the goats.

EVOLUTION

What you see, what you think
what you believe in
evolves.

What you found
so magnificent, those clouds.
Yes, they still are

and the doves could not be
more archetypal on the chimneys.
But the feeling's changed.

It's different, it goes
with another era, another mood
now new, as if 'new' is good.

Moods are like weather
and we all know
what's happened to weather.

WHICH TRUER BE?

That *parfait of selves,* remember?
Sometimes the order shifts—
cream on the bottom, in between
or swirling. *Cut it out!*

As if, as if, as if. But it's OK
to wear hats, as it is clothes
costumes and feathers, as long
as they in some way fit.

When you speak with someone
you don't yet know, you try
to find them where they are
speak their language, so to speak.

It is not false. You still have
your center—even in a chorus
a voice that is singular
gracious, hopefully not too

calculating, socially competent.
My father was an actor
and actors are mimics.
He delighted as he delighted in

most natural pastiche.
I must have acquired some
along with a strange, oppressive
need to put others at ease.

GARDENS

I do not want to care for them.
I don't even want to care about them.
Look, yes, as at someone else's life
and passions, stories planted
long ago—*temps perdu*—
a linden tree more recently.

Newcomers! I hear their laughter
through an open window.
They feel themselves strangers
though won't for long.
Time wears, wearies and settles.
Yet another stray cat will find a home.

I do not want a garden of my own.
Harmonies, yes, an herb or two
little to water, weed or prune
or put to bed at the end of the season.
A winter quilt for chillier nights helps.
Don't force my hand.

SECRETS OF THE SECRET GARDEN

No, we won't try to tame it, as if that were possible.
The claiming may nor may not occur
laws of lands and heirs being what they are.
If ever, it will not be a bourgeoise acquisition
but a wild station in perpetuity.

Brambles may go, slowly, with diligence and gloves.
Bay can stay forever, ever taller—a stew leaf monument.
And lemon balm. *Balm in Gilead.*
The trees beyond their lifetimes will not fall in ours
but become sculptures, Easter Island *au naturel.*

Bones of mammoths, architecture of desire.
There's form and reason. There are secrets with which
to collide, or dismiss. *Nous cherchons,* as if there are answers.
You can never keep up, or keep. (Don't let the cat
eat the vinca.) The secret garden keeps its own.

Now I say...

It was a hot summer night during *confinement*. We were on the little balcony in the back. (I, after all, had insisted on *no garden*.) The bell rang but we didn't hear it, then did, or a furtive knocking or divination led my husband to the front door. The lovely older man who sometimes delivers packages in the evening was there. Perhaps he'd had a another job that had been erased. He indeed had a package for us.

My husband apologized for keeping him waiting, explained that we were upstairs behind the house, our only outdoor reprieve from the heat. Perhaps in attempt to strengthen the excuse I think he presented our situation as a bit woeful. But, the lovely delivery man, working at an hour when he might have begun to watch the stars, replied cheerfully, *"Oui, mais ça existe!"*

Now I say about many things, many times a day, aloud or silently within breath's coven, to cheer or chastise, or both—(though my husband declares there wasn't the faintest note of the latter in the man's voice)—with gratitude or resignation, *Mais ça existe, ça existe, ça existe!*

THE BAT-EARED CAT

A ghostly messenger
whose message I failed to receive.

It was snowing, and I closed the door
long before I saw the homeless man

on 110th with pierced feet.
I don't believe, I don't believe

but jolted in the street.
It couldn't be, glowing in the snow

like radium. A radium tabby
with exorbitant ears flickers still.

I imagine the blizzard swirling
frozen tufts whitening to Dorian Gray.

It was before I knew they come to you
because they think you see.

DETAIL

Her hair was neither long enough to tie back
nor short enough to evade, so she slept in a mass of tangles
sometimes damp at the back of her neck.

The cat, still a kitten, replacement for one who'd gone
as they all do, came and went, stopping near her breath
to nurse on its own paw.

Dreams were out of the question, or only dreams.
What was the point? There were no real complaints
just a few annoying strands of hair across her eyelids

and a body lying very still, trying to notice what it feels.
Is there pain somewhere? *Douleur?* Weight? Redolence?
What would thought beyond a question be?

The bed itself is glorious, always appreciated
warm and cool at once if a limb moves across its silhouette.
She fears abstraction, wanting nothing but particular detail

and detail of detail, to be in the presence of these, if not absorb.
Like the kitten playing with a newly discovered not yet dead fly.
There should be atmosphere too, no?

Nice clouds, almost always, that move with mood, create mood
eradicate with thankful evolution
all detail.

POTION

I've always had one perfect fingernail.
One in ten. The others are OK
but one is perfect, perfectly shaped
a classic no evolution can change.

One in ten isn't bad
for something you get to keep
your whole life, into old age
even as the body ruins

a body, extant but becoming
unimportant, so many things
it can't do—jump rope like a bored kid.
No sing-song potion.

The mind, too, trying to gather
autumnal thoughts into a pile
really just evocation of the body
that had been there.

ATTENTIONS

Not to detail but unavoidable
if fleeting, attention to trivia
associations expanding, surprising.
Do parts become a whole?

Attend the Lords of France and Burgundy, Gloucester.
I saw my father drunk only once
and that's what he said, over and over
almost sang. His role, many years ago.

What is magic but more than a wish
with 'reality' so pedestrian?
A creature lives, a creature dies
or many creatures. All of us.

Naturally or unnaturally. Or
what seems bizarre and unnatural—
war, assault, murder—is actually
natural, for humans and others.

I wish, I wish, I wish for enchantment
for certainty, something beyond
the painful abstraction of language
when one tries to speak beyond stone.

When it's your turn, will you be able
to speak beyond sorrow, or at all
some truth or untold story
sheltered or forgotten.

*

I'm living up here with the birds.
Almost literally. It happens to be
the tallest building in the village
minus the never-completed cathedral.

Now I see dove courtship. The male
(they say) taking a deep bow, once, twice
again. Then walking away. I am living
with the doves. Pigeons, no?

Ring-necked and elegant, they coo
in phrases that cannot be reproduced.
Standing on the church roof, almost eye level
gray against gray roof and sky

they coo and coo and coo until the brain
resigns, and you don't hear them.
I'm living with the swifts too.
They fly and fly, morning and evening

insane aerodynamics, shrieks and squeals.
The bats are silent. Why is 'attention'
something that must be 'paid'?
Attend the lords of France and Burgundy, Gloucester!

RUSSET

They went russet this year, terse and heedless
except for the ivy, and that's about all.
Those beautifully groomed French forests
where *sanglier* wander and snort
(though I've yet to see one up-close).

Some yellow and gold, none bright, no real red.
Not New England, not glowing.
What is there to count on if not color?
One wants the real thing. One wants a real
something, dicey or sublime—Autumn!

Or was that childhood, irreproducible.

WINTER GREEN

I like winter—chilly and gray
and endless. Complaints
are endless, a lifestyle. No one
is expected to be happy
or allowed.

Even the lettuce is tough
even in the 'Garden of France'.
Arugula, bitter to begin with
is bitterer still, dirt on the celery
hard to get off, not

the gentle crumbs of summer.
It's tough winter dirt. Eat it!
Along with things you might not
in abundance—all those roots

and other pale things.
Except the parsley is green
very very dark green, inky
green, curled like wooly coronets
of unshorn sheep. Tough

and *blessed* (in the vernacular).
I like winter warmth under
a mountain of sweaters
kin to a stuffed animal
blissfully slow, or frankly

immobile, without obligations
with a view of fog, remote
outline of a town, a whole planet
you know is there
but can ignore.

Le Concert des Oiseaux
(The Concert of the Birds)

It was an assemblage from old to new
Purcell to Saint-Saëns, Couperin to Ravel
with a viola de gamba and theorbe, no less.

Enchanting OK, I hear them, but I hear them
every morning, the real ones. After first light
has brought the cat to nuzzle, suck on her paw

the birds come. A lone *tweet* at first, as if
waiting, unsure, then another bold *chirp*
or many, the doves alto, *whoo, cheep.*

Charm, demand, demanding a day
the light almost invisible. Be full-throated
for the day. Be sure-footed, fly.

I used to curse the birds, turn and groan
forced awake. That was then. Now I just listen.
A song or a howl, someone else's music

destiny or day. A world outside a window.
Who can touch, children, remnants, fierce
impenetrable happiness, unhappiness for which

there are only the most particular notes.
Remind me why we needed to go so far
as to call nature, *nature,* something other

than what we are, so far from a simple
irrevocable glimmer of light, the kitten
nursing like an infant, *le concert des oiseaux.*

Make music, make love, something
other than hate, war, blighted oceans
centuries of righteous human dross.

Now a sad bird, yet peaceful and melodious
perhaps prophetic. A short song, perhaps
the light came too late. When is dawning

ever timely or sufficient? One bird
apologizes for another, enhances
devours the orchestral score

one bird, anonymous as they are
counted as many, a chorus. One bird
with wings beyond melody.

ARPEGGIO

They've returned again.
I can see them now
across the slate and terracotta
but less well these years later
eyes less suited for discerning.

But yes, more certainly than ever
they're crows, harder to recognize
in their modesty.

Yes, even crows are modest
high above their critics
busy with what must be called
family life, flutteringly at peace.

If they're cawing, I'm too far
or deaf to hear.

If they're stealing, I say
take the whole lot.

If murdering, let me give you
a list.

II

Lose the Scent

SUNDAY

What could possibly be important at this moment—
urgency or eternity, or will they meet?

So many travesties, large and small.
Some get smaller as others grow huge.

So much pain. Is death pain or the end of pain?
In the worst plague, almost half lived.

Maybe like pruning hydrangea, not enough resource
for us old folks anyway. What urgency, cruelty

seems to have existed for eternity?
We live in *a dream within a dream* of radical denial

about to be chastened. So many plans!
But, will I be dead before the end of this line?

I know it can happen. It happened to someone I knew
strolling on his favorite trail on Sunday.

No one dies on Sunday
because everyone's at brunch.

ON THE NATURE OF CREATURES

What kind are we really? Not kind
not the kind kind, if there is such.
We love and long, desire and groan
empty the seas and the forests.

Predator, prey, kill or dismiss?
Victim, victimizer, what contempt
hurts most? Can there be a simple life
for all, if water? If not drowning in water?

A creature I love kills other different
creatures I love. Sadistically sometimes
eats them sometimes. We kill them all, too.
We do, all. And our sad own.

OFFICIAL WINE DIARY FOR AFFICIONADOS

Sour and bitter
with notes of fuel oil.
Officious. Yes, they're
really just moods.

I like mine bland
pale, plain, clear liqs only
as before surgery, as long
as there's ETOH.

I experimented once, in a chemistry lab.
No, the hangover doesn't come
from acids and aldehydes.
It comes from the real thing.

Some make you sing:
As a pilgrim I did go
to a land that I did know
to the shores of Trist la Cal

to see if I still felt the say-aa-aim.
And the sun blazed madly insane.
Wasn't that Donovan?
Is he still alive?

THE PATIENT

The more I try to sympathize
with you, the more it offends.
Why? Why is that?

Because it's only about you
you contemplating your defeat.

Not your guard? Your rage?
Torture by inconsolability?
So grandiose.

(I once knew someone who
thought it was *grand-doe-ease.*)

Whose vanity is whose?
Whose need to succeed or fail
in seduction of the wounded feral.

SIMPLICITY

I want to live poor. Not *poor* poor
but rich with modesty, a passion for surcease:
a couple of sweaters, cotton and worn
to a fine sheen. A few nice vegetables

an occasional oyster from the sea.
One pair of earrings and maybe one more.
A steaming shower many days—extravagant
perhaps shameful, but *ahhh*.

A cat, of course, a pencil and
the sharpest sharpener. An address without
flood, fire, plague, war, if these could be
commanded like commandments.

No parties, just strolls, maybe a glass
of local something, sometimes, surely
with a friend, or kind stranger.
Cotton and worn while the world goes on

and on and on or maybe not.
I want to visit the elephant graveyard
bones mingled with the dinosaurs'.
They were my friends, though nobody knew.

AUTEUR

When I am safely here
my arms exhausted from rowing.

I'll tell you who is speaking—
auteur, a voice that may not be

a voice at all, a distant harmony
Yes, there is water—wide, troubled

biblical water. *Troubled* here is
good, I hope you know...

Safety will be when
the dogs lose the scent.

WHEN YOU'RE...

...in a foreign country
the country is not foreign, *you* are.

You're the foreigner.
You belong elsewhere, perhaps only

in your own skin, somewhere.
You belong everywhere and nowhere.

Skin of cream or gold, anthracite
touch me. Let us touch each other.

Languages may make no sense
even one's own, to oneself.

Trill on the high notes, universal
utterance. Speak clearly.

GERRYMANDER

The cat *is* a metaphor, and comic relief.
I write cat poems to have something soft
to touch, something silly and furry, with
their own lovingly inconsequential dignity.

Why should there not be paradox, this
feeling and that contradiction, the sorrow
and the loss, the rage and the glee, envy
even of what looks to some like poverty.

How endlessly we need, are we allowed
to look away? No, never... But, if your own home
is full of love and if you're black in America
how good that love may be—everything.

Does a poem need structure? Is that a stupid
question? Or, imperative? Language alone
is anatomy. The more important, the most
important question is, do *we* need structure

armature to believe in, some way to behave
and poetry to rehearse, envision, retrieve?
Did Hart Crane jump, no not off a bridge
but to his death, into Marianne Moore's sea

because of beautiful, not-yet-in-fashion
fashionable desire? And did Bishop, I
get it, want to be unfree? All ghettos
are crowded. Is rage like an infection that

every known cure has stopped working
against? And, did the Girl Scouts not let me
join, just accidently, so they said, because
my mother was in the asylum?

SHE IS ELEVEN

She is eleven.
She likes to paint on old wood
as in a medieval church—
roses and tulips and things.
(From where do these anachronisms come?)

She's hungry and scared. Maybe not scared—
bold creature. She is with her grandmother
her mother does not know where.
Eleven and pretty as a flower, too pretty.
Her mother is trembling.

She's hiding with neighbors and strangers.
The shelter walls sweat because they're hot
or cold, you can't tell which.
They're under, way under the earth
a sanctuary near purgatory.

Some of the strangers are soldiers.
Their thick fabric stinks
like their bodies. You cannot tell
if they're afraid, if their sweat
is hot or cold.

Neighbors closer than you've ever
seen them. Soup from potatoes
stored in the cellar, thankfully.
No water to wash them, the dirt
is rubbed to a fine patina

like a medieval painting.
She will be rescued. Yes, her mother
found her, a mother more terrified
than the soldier about to sleep
eternally in the dirt.

She'll be 12 and 13, paint on old wood
go to school in another country.
They'll like her because she's
pretty, without a language
but with fierce eyes.

JUSTICE

Do not go to war.
Do not go. Do not be
a country or a soldier
a stray animal or a corpse
a refugee left hungry or drowned.

Do not pretend
assault or invasion is 'war'.
Do not go to war for
justice. There is no just war
just war.

Or blow the entire sorry planet
to prehistoric eternity—
no breath to be taken again
by or from anyone.
No wind, no cinders.

No war. Absolution.
Did he who made the lamb
make thee?

BOOMERS

Maybe it's just old people
who think it's over
because it nearly is, for us.

Or the strange illusion-delusion
of that postwar America
of hope. That era of all

doors open, effortless hope.
And we did it, and lived it
made long dead immigrant

grandparents proud, their
sacrifice and modesty, hope itself
beyond measure. We did it:

college, affluence, titles
greed, therapy, TJMaxx, pet
therapy, Bergdorf's. And now

is there smog in London again?
Drought somewhere we can
can barely name?

Now *the pitiless wave.*
When 'war' is the name
for assault. Has it always been?

Ignorant, impressionistic
I guess it's always been.
O God, Can I not save/ One...

Or is it now overly knowing
the world as we do or do not
every corner of avarice

and sorrow, values that value
what about our nature
we did not wish to know.

Modesty

We have too much.
We want too much.
Cherish your privation.
It makes you better.

Cherish and do not
abrogate the beauty of living
by the weight of a songbird
or the wind that sounds like one.

2022

Only out of tenderness are you so raw
of a humor that may not even be funny.

Too much tenderness, too much.
The pain simple or shattering, or internal

in the light of a fragile soul, cautious or flawed.
There's no time for all, if there's time for any.

I did not want the dog to bite me, to tear my face.
I did not want my mother to suicide or die in childbirth.

She says, at least there was a loving wet nurse.
What can even the most loving breast

do for civilizations crumbling? What small consolation
cheering what righteousness, the small beauty

of a plum or a pear on a windowsill
overlooking Hell. Only out of tenderness

does the array of choices bewilder beyond
any eventuality or consent. Only out of tenderness

is there an ethical choice, the sorrow that trails
the hearse, the widow who flees the coffin

to a new life. Tenderness remains, what?
Something human before we were the way we are.

Also

We're not just bowing to catastrophe.
There's also great joy, and small—
that bowl of soup with noodles floating
happily.

France just beat the Brits (hooray!)
and the streets are wild, as they should be.
(Pray there won't be mayhem when they play
Morocco.)

There's the comfort of antiques
and old friends, antiques too
who smile knowingly, world weary
and content.

Animals are easier and easier to love
and those who love them. What fun to have
a hedgehog bathed and whispered to
in Italian.

A dog licking the cat's nose.
My husband entwined with a goose.
The cat curled against me, sucking
her furry thumb.

Everything to see and see—
beautiful vegetables and beautiful leaves.
Cars honking and singing in the streets.
Bells and poetry.

THE ARTISTS SURVIVE BECAUSE THEY HAVE SOMETHING TO DO

When the blight got so bad
it was in our bones, it was us.

Warring, hateful, vengeful.
Thirsty. Hot and dry.
The animals were hot and dry.

Greed brought no one
more than superficial riches.

Believe me, I know them.
I know their children.
They had much, everything.
But they did not have good lives.

What can be said to Charon?
Whose language might be understood?

There used to be friendship.
We thought we were all friends.

Now there are tepid cries
small optimisms, accommodation
shaking silly thoughts away.

The day is beautiful.
Nasturtiums are surviving still
colors of The Renaissance
sustaining, if anything is.

BLUES

Somewhere between slate and cobalt
with a blast of light within. There.

Where? Where is the sky? Not a place
but a moment, like any other.

Love the blue now, while you can
see it, before it's eclipsed by fire

emolliated, and swept into clouds
silenced among the planets.

The dark cloud is a companion.

III

SECOND BLOOM

BEGIN

We're waiting for the season
yet it's begun. We're waiting with
great anticipation, and it's nearly over.
The cherries. How ripe, how fast.
The birds gorged! Strawberries
a long running sigh from the south.
No, not nectarines already, zucchini
to clog the pipes, forward movement
and I don't know what.
Asparagus was subtle and long ago
now just feathers before the season
we weren't ready for. Is it now?
Is it now? Is it? Yes, it's now.

SECOND BLOOM

> *Rose, oh pure contradiction: Desire,*
> *to be no-one's sleep under so many lids.*
> —Rainer Maria Rilke (tr), on his tombstone

The first was explosive, a convocation
one could barely breathe.

Now, I take you gently.
I know the size of your weapons, large and small.

I know how to avoid them, or don't care.
A thorn, a tacit injury. Neither masochism nor stigmata

but unity, a barter for astonishment.
They keep coming and coming, small from the dry

this dry earth of a dry planet. Small but mighty?
No, just fragrant, some, or one.

I think of Rilke writing near his death, of roses.
How much a sweet ascent? In French, no less.

The mystery of this own epitaph—none other would do?
How stunningly self-contained!

There's exegesis
(which sounds like a cross between *exhume* and *explain*).

There are pages and theses. My husband says
"I (meaning himself) have something better to do."

I (meaning myself) think there's nothing better.
Vitally, know, just know, the petals revered

the thorns reviled, translations irrelevant.
There was and is no mystery. Forgive him, no poetry.

He simply did not want to die, told the rose to go on living.
Effigy, amulet, fetish back to youth in Worpswade:

Rose, oh reiner Widerspruch, Lust,
Niemandes Schlaf zu sein unter soviel Lidern.

I'm going to write it down, all versions
in a thousand languages. Mediate upon it

like a mantra, use it like a Rorschach, a cat toy
an ambulance, a fountain, a salad.

*

The petals I exchange in the waterglass
every few days, the new surprise as we old folks
shake our heads, hang our heads.

Petals no sentiment no metaphor
watching the peach and the rose and the red
bearing their thorns like crowns.

Please tell me they're not the true fruit.
Speak to me, flower. No they do not.
There's no meaning in beauty.

There may not even be beauty in beauty.
There's fact. Thorn of fact.
Not nihilism, realism. Scent and barb.

Please slice to some truth, any, that will last.
Admiring your defense, brilliant.
Admiring my respect, with wounds.

*

The secret garden is not a secret anymore.
Not an overgrown parking lot
in which a ghetto house tumbled or burned.
Not a roadside tavern. Just space that
no one wants to own or give up.
Just a place to come out of the depths
disillusioned but unscathed, as if place
defines us beyond skin, without ignorance.
The secret garden owns me, owns us, in ruins.
To say one likes 'nature' is as if speaking
in a world in which we're long gone.

*

You must not understand
words do not matter
neither yours nor mine.
Ancient testaments
to meaning.

We are in flight
but cannot fly.
The birds are in flight
but they cannot land.

We cannot love
what we've failed to love
anymore.

*

Accommodating the sun
the heart, skillfully.
Whispering all the while
I'm glad I'm old.
Having lived nicely
even with madnesses.

Beautiful sky here today
through gauze curtains
not quite the end
but we can see the end
or only our silly elder ends

so beautiful through the gauze?
Is the moon waxing or waning?
Who knows! Details.
Anoint someone who knows.

*

Maybe the thorns are more important than the rose.
Now let's be honest, they are, now.

Their certainty, durability, their form, arched
like an invasion of the past, and the future.

*

Julie said the rose comes with the thorns (or mistyped, *thrones*).
She said it, apparently, many times, in many ways
spellbound that the petals, the scents, come with thorns.
Isn't it interesting, she said, our most cherished flower...

Coronation of the rose, crowning like an infant's head emerging.
Crown the rose. The promise of the rose focuses all on a flower
that comes with a thorn. (I hate metaphor. I want only the actual
unembellished: *A rose is a rose is a rose is a rose by any other name...*)

*

Not like the shade under a fig tree
whose genital-shrouding bear paws
flap and fan the ripe scent, or inflame
because they have many lives, sheltering
the doves who can still find a drop
in the *ruisseau,* or growing through
chopping and mowing and stone.

Dementia Again

Not that scent again.
Not linden. No, jasmine
must be.

Or, farther away.
Are clouds scented, are stars?
What do I not remember

or whom?
The word or the thought
of the moment.

There's only this scent
all encompassing, nameless
cruel.

SPEAKING FRENCH AGAIN

The old woman has forgotten I do not understand her easily.
Yet she speaks easily as I try to ask twice or thrice, if she's well.
She says *oui,* though I know it not to be entirely true.

I can see it, the time gone by. Yet she's one of the few left.
Another, incoherent is cared for elsewhere. Others you never
would have suspected, have left. This is the natural course

in our small village, the rains, the fields. Those who came before
going as the lovely bells continue to strike. These are the words
we didn't learn, or did not say, but understood.

Her daughter visits frequently, friendly now, converses with our cat.
Familiar as neighbors come to be. *If your mother ever needs anything...*
silently or in the incoherent babble of good cheer.

A True Tale

Saving the paper from a lovely gift I
put down the ribbon and it disappeared.
A true tale of straying, or inebriation.
Where, where, where did it go?
A few seconds later, a lifetime ago?
Who cares? The trivial owns you.
You try so hard to get it right
like in the old days when you got
many things right, by effort, anxiety
force of nature, good luck, etc.
Now it's all about *integrity vs. despair*
the last of the last about which you'll
be able to care. And, who gives a shit
about saving the wrapping anyway?
Waste not want not. No string too short...
During the depression we...
Turn your head, turn and turn, laugh
or weep for centuries, senility.
The cat is playing with it on the stairs.

My Blurb

Salut, c'est moi, Gisèle!

This is my first blurb! I'm so excited! Because she's plum outa poets, friends, literary anybody, Lauri asked me. Me-meow!

Her husband is funny. I like him. He doesn't want much to do with poetry because he doesn't "want it to come between them." Weird, huh?

But he'll sometimes listen to one or two, shake his head or unintentionally chuckle appropriately at something intentional. He says some are fluffy, like meringue, and that one long one was "poetic waterboarding". Plus there's alota "caboosing"—bright red digressions always bumping you from behind (or bumping your behind) for no reason. Or, that she keeps adding extra, random, free-associated, TMI, overly inclusive, histrionic, distracting, jerky cars on the poor train for no reason. Today he said, "Whatever it is, I think it's still hiding in the rushes."

I say, *What what what chaff?*—process itself the dance, its ragged self.

But, this is a nice book. You'll like it. (tt is a super fine designer!)

And, I'm cute too. I have saucer eyes like a 60's Keane poster. *Mignon,* like they say in France, like filet mignon. *Délicieux!* Maybe I'll get a bite someday.

Love,
Gisèle

The Funeral Parlor Next to the Bar

The funeral parlor next to the bar
is for sale. Actually, the bar is too.

Where the dead once lay undisturbed
and undisturbing.

"...the reason for living was to get ready to stay dead a long time."

It's been a long time.
I doubt the scent of formaldehyde

or death is extant—putrescine.
Not even the fruit of the vine.

Though a certain scent is always there
anticipating the incomprehensible

the thing you really may need God for—
passing the baton, the centuries

that speak or bleed through
pamplisest or pentimento.

The windows are fogged, practically glazed.
Signs are in foreign emoji, the traffic too close.

No one remembers being there.
The funeral parlor next to the bar—

you can go from torpor to stupor
to eternity.

BEAUTY

It grays, it grays, whitens in a stripe
so at last I can look like Susan Sontag.

Whom did you think women coming of age
in the seventies wanted to look like?

Someone smart. Younger than Simone
de Beauvoir, less obscure Veil or Weil.

Though always an unfettered feminist
I have a confession to make:

It was and is obvious, women want
to be beautiful. Say it raw, I have always...

Such is life, full of shallow and hollow.
Never hideous but now it all seems silly.

Is presentable enough?
"Pretty enough for all normal purposes."

Are you pretty enough to play yourself
in the movie version? Or, as we know

or should, deeply in our bones
beauty is made of dignity, unimaginable

and complex. I wanted to look like...
I used to want, women want.

I stared in the mirror, sucked in my cheeks.
Beautiful like a Burne-Jones, youngish

Vanessa Redgrave, sad Garbo. Now
all I want is to be alive.

ANOTHER FOR JOHANNA

Why should I remember now
or any time, she made dressing
with the tomatoes themselves.

I remember now, in tomato season
and taste, forever trying for perfection.
They say it's a bad year, chilly and wet.

There's blight unless the wind sears
through to dry them. Her dressing
so different than mine with vinegars

and lemon, the true fruit of the vine.
(As kids we sucked on them like peaches.
No wonder our teeth have no enamel.)

How different her life—pure courage.
Yes, there really is such a thing.
And joy, in making, being, love

a dog and an immigrant's arrival.
When the doctor asked what she wanted
she said, "I want to live." As if it was

a choice, pure, and strangely oblivious
to trenchant realities that make
the rest of us tremble in our small lives.

TIRED

Tired of convention.
Tired of aging, being old.
Even I, consoled by the familiar
am tired of a small life, of being small.

For years I loved the chocolate bar
with hazelnuts, dark and brimming
Now, I'm tired of it.

Is it melancholy, or a lesson about novelty?
Almonds seem novel now, once again
and a twice-as-expensive sesame bar.

Tired of fire and war. Look at us, look!
Tired of the empty-headed bourgeoise
height-of-Western-civilization way of living.
But then, I tired of it long ago.

Tired of repetition, tired tired tired.
The last word, and the first.

All words, languages, extremes, poisonous
plants, viruses, fire and flood, death, cruelty
lists, listlessness, alliteration
hope and platitudes.

What are all those
fuzzy-looking things out there?
Trees? Well, I'm tired
of them...

THE GHOST HOUSE

And I am the ghost, never living here
though arranged it meticulously
a little paradise no one can touch.

My home's across the ocean, the song goes.
My home is in the ocean, the middle
between continents, perhaps once joined.

My home is everywhere and nowhere
the way some people love everyone
and no one all at once.

All to be given up anyway.
Things only images, images only thoughts.
Habitation ephemeral as afternoon sheen.

Do the rooms of any house hold us?
If you're lucky enough… How to live
with beautiful old wood, more living

than the sad, bewildered body
that cannot locate itself
the precious ghost who polished it so.

The trees are tall and yellow in October
as beautiful as happenstance. I'm sad
because I know I'll never live here

or will because you're dead.
But keep it pristine, for the swap needed
when I return too decrepit to remain.

THE EMPTY ROOM

Why do I like an empty room?
Not completely empty: a table, a chair
a bowl of tangerines, something reminiscent
of life uncluttered, only attention to sustain.
Floors and walls, a fireplace, curtains fluttering
down the hall, stone geometries next door
almost too much to bear.

Not a love of emptiness
but something spare, with time
and space to think. There is so little time
and who would dare to think?

What is small peace? Can you keep it clean
with little effort? Can you mend it?
What will outlast you? Not yourself!
The brick and mortar? What will be grateful
for your care? Tangerines in a spun glass bowl?
Is an empty room a preview
or from where we came?

INCANTATIONS
for Tom Duffy (1937-2022)

When the mortal uncoils its skinny folds
is this all death is, absence from an unmade bed?
Can I blame whom I miss on the air
the fog, the mist, what memory is?

Let me go, let me, if I have to go, let go.

When the mortal uncoils its flimsy profusion
Goodbye is something we don't know how to say
until it is said. Please teach me.

*

I do not need a funeral.
I do not need a shroud.
Nor flowers nor velvet.
Not even song.
Especially not song.

*

When the mortal uncoils
like Kekulé's snake letting go of its tail
no molecule to discover
I'll love you still.

Presence still enough
breath still enough
still enough.

*

He crossed 'the rainbow bridge' last night
for those of us who like metaphors.
Of course I like metaphors, but not for death.
Nor euphemisms. Please don't say
passed, passed away, passed on, departed, perished, left
succumbed, called back, gone home, away, journey's end
eternal rest. Say *died, dead, death.* Please.

*

You knew what was coming.
You knew and, of course, couldn't know.
The hospital bed wheeled in unceremoniously
anathema. The drops and the chants
visitors in cloaks or the dreadfully cheery.
You knew, you doctor of doctors, you.
Doctor who wrote the books, now forced
foreseen, to write your own.
Begging to leave and begging to stay.
Not like this, but not wanting to end, to slip
like a word on the tongue, to drain
the color, the mien, the sound uncoiled.

*

The hand on the back is aged.
The hand on the aged back.
Time heals. Time wounds all.
Why is that?

Do some good on this earth
if there is good to be done.
There is comfort. There is comfort.
The good is done.

Not Unexpected

But never expected.
The heart never trusts

a double negative.
The heart never wants

compromises, each decrement.
Please stay, please

do not go, please do not
let this day

be the end of days.
Never ready, begging to be

ready, begging for never.
No peace. No no no

peace. Yes, there is
but not for the living.

The immortal coil
memory, more graceful

than death, death
more graceful than living.

How to count
its turns.

It Doesn't Last

Not the fabric, not the document
the idea, or the wood
even the stone.
Neither the style nor the beloved
cat. Not the beloved. Not you
corporeal or even the so-called soul.
No, not the ragged body.
Not the body politic (thankfully).
Not even the species that did not change
before extinction.

BARELY

Barely sun
but I don't mind
for a day or two, a season or two.
Let the clouds be beautiful, ever advancing
as all is, the half-life of metaphor expiring.
Admit gray is balm
if not reason.

Notes

I

Attentions

Apple Tree
Their weight carries no gravity; Allusion to Isaac Newton's discovery of gravity.

Between
Go Down Moses; https://en.wikipedia.org/wiki/Go_Down_Moses.

Which Truer Be?
parfait of selves; As if, as if, as if. Associations to LR, "In the Cave Redux" & "As If", *An Æsthetic of Stone.*

Gardens
temps perdu; Allusion to Marcel Proust, *À la recherche du temps perdu.*

Secrets of The Secret Garden
Association to LR, "The Secret Garden", *Après.*
Balm in Gilead; https://en.wikipedia.org/wiki/Balm_of_Gilead
Easter Island; https://en.wikipedia.org/wiki/Easter_Island
Don't let the cat/ eat the vinca; https://www.aspca.org/pet-care/animal-poison-control/toxic-and-non-toxic-plants/vinca

Now I say...
confinement; Mandatory stay-at-home in France during the pandemic 2020.

The Bat-eared Cat
the homeless man on 110th with pierced feet; https://en.wikipedia.org/wiki/Homeless_Jesus
Dorian Gray; https://en.wikipedia.org/wiki/The_Picture_of_Dorian_Gray

Attentions
Attend the Lords of France and Burgundy, Gloucester; William Shakespeare,
King Lear, Act 1, Scene 1.

Winter Green
'Garden of France'—Reference to the Loire Valley.

Arpeggio
Association to LR, "Birthday Poem", *An Æsthetic of Stone.*

II
LOSE THE SCENT

Sunday
In the worst plague, almost half lived; https://en.wikipedia.org/wiki/List_
of_epidemics
a dream within a dream; Edgar Allan Poe, "A Dream Within A Dream".

Official Wine Diary for Afficionados
*As a pilgrim I did go/ to a land that I did know/ to the shores of Trist la Cal/
to see if I still felt the say-aa-aim./*
And the sun blazed madly insane; Donovan, "Belated Forgiveness Plea",
Fairytale, 1965; https://www.youtube.com/watch?v=HUPlKpcK85w

Auteur
When I am safely here/my arms exhausted from rowing; Association to LR,
"The Secret Garden, Woke", *Après.*
lose the scent; Troubled; https://en.wikipedia.org/wiki/Wade_in_the_Water

Gerrymander
The cat is a metaphor; Association to LR, "The Unifanger", "No, the cat is
not...", *Après.*

78

Justice
Did he who made the lamb/ make thee? William Blake, "The Tyger".

Boomers
the pitiless wave; O God, Can I not save/ One...; Edgar Allan Poe, "A Dream Within a Dream".

Also
France just beat the Brits; https://en.wikipedia.org/wiki/2022_FIFA_World_Cup.

The Artists Survive Because They Have Something To Do
Charon; https://en.wikipedia.org/wiki/Charon

III
SECOND BLOOM

Second Bloom
The secret garden; Association to LR, "The Secret Garden", *Après;* "Secrets of The Secret Garden" (above).
A rose is a rose is a rose is a rose by any other name...; https://en.wikipedia.org/wiki/Rose_is_a_rose_is_a_rose_is_a_rose; https://en.wikipedia.org/wiki/A_rose_by_any_other_name_would_smell_as_sweet

Dementia Again
Reference to LR, "Dementia", *Après.*

Speaking French Again
Reference to LR, "Speaking French", *An Æsthetic of Stone.*
A True Tale
integrity vs. despair; https://en.wikipedia.org/wiki/Erikson%27s_stages_of_psychosocial_development

My Blurb
process itself the dance; vague allusion to *How can we know the dancer from the dance?* "Among School Children", William Butler Yeats.
Keane poster; https://en.wikipedia.org/wiki/Margaret_Keane

The Funeral Parlor Next to the Bar
"...the reason for living was to get ready to stay dead a long time."; William Faulkner, *As I Lay Dying.*

Beauty
Veil or Weil; https://en.wikipedia.org/wiki/Simone_Veil; https://en.wikipedia.org/wiki/Simone_Weil
"Pretty enough for all normal purposes."; Thornton Wilder, *Our Town,* Act I.

Another for Johanna
Reference to LR, "Johanna", *An Æsthetic of Stone;* "This is What Memory Is", *Where Do the Memories Go?*

Tired
What are all those/ fuzzy-looking things out there?/ Trees? Well, I'm tired/ of them...; William Carlos Williams, "The Last Words of My English Grandmother".

Incantation (& Not Unexpected)
Allusions to the mortal coil; https://en.wiktionary.org/wiki/mortal_coil
Kekulé's snake; https://en.wikipedia.org/wiki/August_Kekulé

It Doesn't Last
the body politic; https://en.wikipedia.org/wiki/Body_politic

LAURI ROBERTSON has written poetry for many years—Adrienne Rich was her mentor. *Ça Existe!* (It Exists!) is her 5th monograph. Lauri is a psychiatrist and psychoanalyst, formerly on the clinical faculty of Yale Medical School. She lives in New Haven, CT and Pontlevoy, France.

9 781959 556398